Planes
AND HOW THEY WORK

Jennifer Prior

Reviewed by John Goldfluss, pilot, and
Alan J. Cross, engineer.

Table of Contents

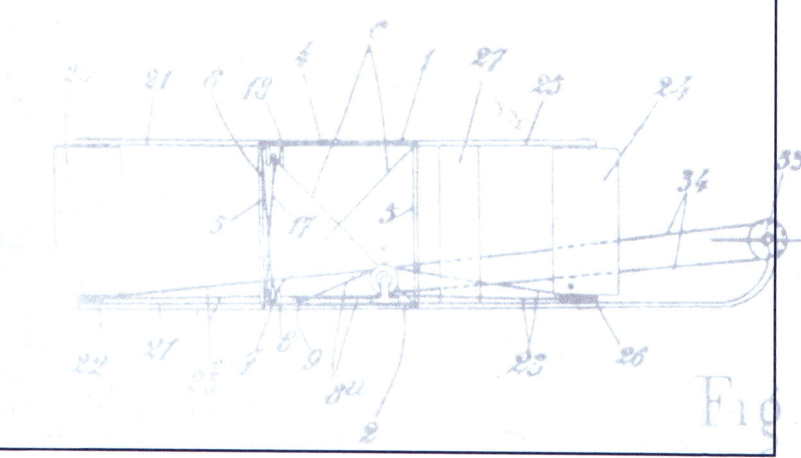

Airplane

Airplane, airplane, up so high,
Flying through the clear blue sky,
Floating on the gentle breeze,
Soaring, soaring, with such ease.

A Brief History of Planes

Have you ever watched a bird and wished you could fly? It seems that people have always dreamed of flying. In fact, as early as the 1800s, people tried to make flying machines.

So, what would be a good model for a plane? You might think that a bird's body would be the best *model*. Many people tried this. However, machines made in this way did not work.

What Is It?

Model is a word with many meanings. Here it means an object that is used as a plan for something else that will be built.

Flight Time Line

Here are some of the important events in flight history.

1793	1853	July 2, 1900
The first hot-air balloon is flown.	The first glider is flown.	The first Zeppelin is flown.

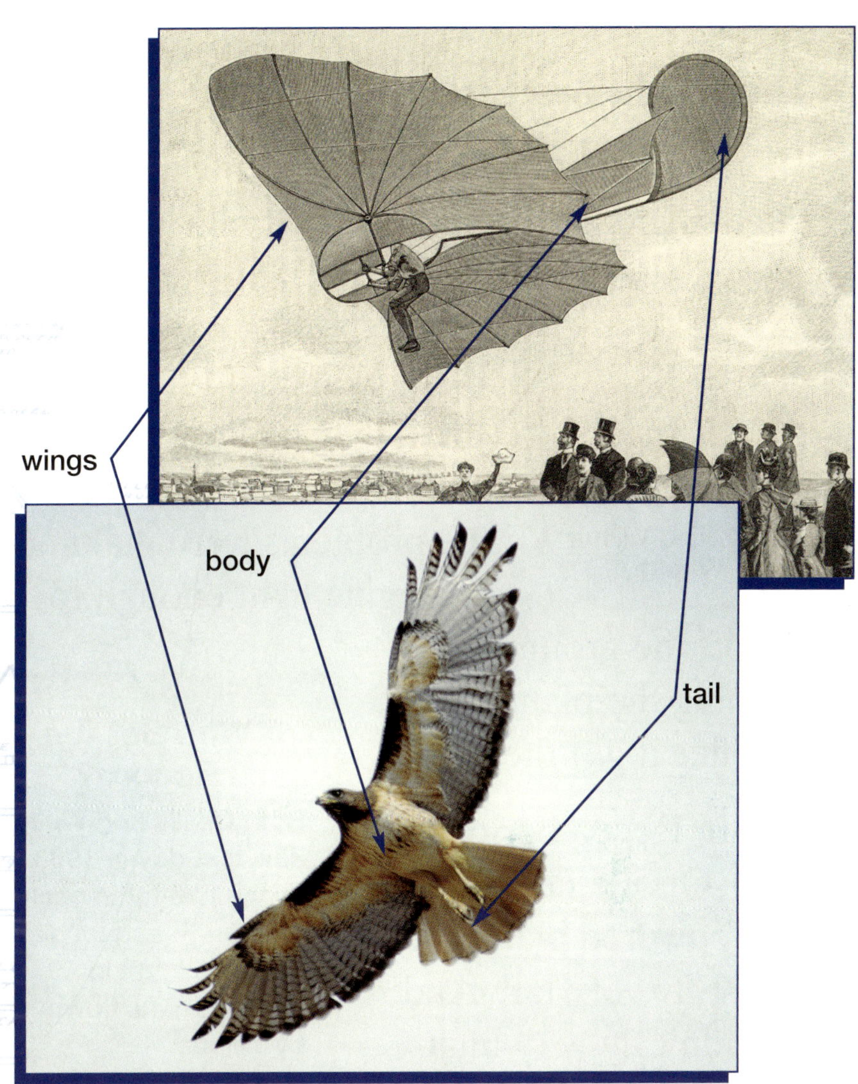

December 17, 1903	November 13, 1907	July 25, 1909
The Wright Brothers make the first flight in an airplane.	The first helicopter is flown.	Louis Blériot is the first to fly across the English Channel.

The Wright Brothers

It was two brothers who finally made the flying dream come true. Orville and Wilbur Wright were the first to build a powered plane that could really fly. First, they had some problems to solve. Two of the problems were making an engine light enough to get off the ground and keeping the plane in the air once it got there!

▲ Orville and Wilbur ▲ Wright

In December of 1903, Orville flew the first powered plane. He didn't fly very far. And he didn't fly very high. But he did fly!

Who Set the Record?

Both Orville and Wilbur flew that day in 1903, taking two turns each. The fourth and longest flight, 852 feet in 59 seconds, was flown by Wilbur.

October 1909	September 1911	December 10, 1911
Elise de Laroche of France becomes the first female pilot.	The first air mail in the U.S. is carried.	Cal Rodgers makes the first flight across a continent.

In later years, the airplane was improved. It was able to carry more people. It could also fly farther.

The First to Fly?

The Wright Brothers were not the first to soar through the air. Hot-air balloons and gliders had been flown before. But the brothers were the first to fly a powered, manned, heavier-than-air, controlled airplane. That was an amazing feat!

▼ Orville Wright flew the first successful manned flight in 1903.

March 1, 1912	June 15, 1921	May 9, 1926
Albert Berry makes the first parachute jump from a powered airplane.	Bessie Coleman becomes the first African-American pilot.	Richard Byrd and Floyd Bennett are the first to fly over the North Pole.

Charles Lindbergh

When planes were first used, they were only flown over land. The distance an airplane could travel had increased, but planes still were not able to fly far, far away. In 1927 that changed. A plane was flown across the ocean by a man named Charles Lindbergh (LIND-burg).

Lindbergh flew a plane from New York to Paris, France. The trip took more than 33 hours to complete. He made the whole trip without ever sleeping. In order to stay awake, Lindbergh put

Amelia Earhart

In 1928, Amelia Earhart became the first woman to fly across the Atlantic Ocean. In 1932, she flew it in a record 14 hours and 56 minutes! She died in 1937 while trying to fly around the world.

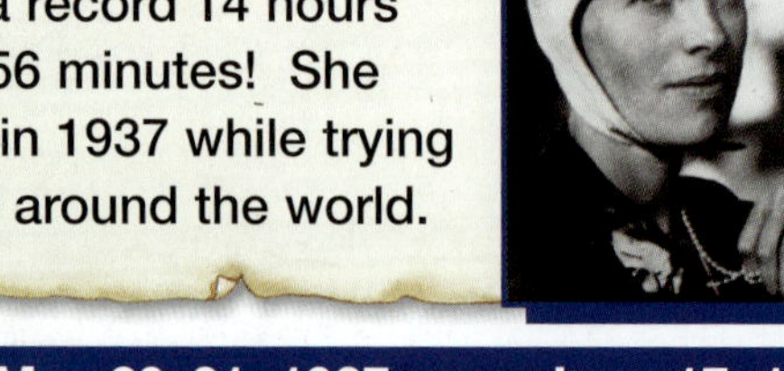

◀ Amelia Earhart

May 20–21, 1927	June 17, 1928	May 15, 1930
Charles Lindbergh makes the first nonstop solo flight across the Atlantic Ocean.	Amelia Earhart becomes the first woman to cross the Atlantic Ocean	Ellen Church becomes the first flight attendant ever to fly.

▲ Charles Lindbergh

Lucky Lindy

Lindbergh was very popular. People called him "Lucky Lindy." His fame helped to spread the word about planes and make them popular, too. Lindbergh also worked hard to improve planes and plane flight.

his head out the window to get a blast of cold air on his face.

When he made it to Paris, there was a big celebration. After the flight, he became a hero, and airplane travel was forever changed.

December 1, 1935	December 17, 1935	1936
The first air traffic control center begins operating.	The first successful passenger airliner takes off for the first time.	The first pressurized cabin plane is built.

Commercial Flight

The *military* was the first group to use planes widely. Some planes were used in World War I. But, major use was made of them in World War II.

After World War II, there were many planes not being used. So, they were used for *commercial* (kuh-MER-shuhl) reasons. People began to travel by plane for long distances instead of taking trains.

1939	September 16, 1947	October 14, 1947
The first jet plane is flown.	The United States Air Force is established.	Charles Yeager is the first to fly faster than the speed of sound.

By the 1950s, planes were very popular. They were used more for long-distance travel than any other kind of transportation.

▼ An airstrip and airplane in the 1950s

March 2, 1949	1956	1969
The first nonstop flight around the world is made.	The first air traffic accident occurs over Arizona.	The first manned spaceship is flown to and lands on the moon.

How Planes Work

Have you ever wondered just how such a big machine can get off the ground? It really is quite amazing. The answer is *aerodynamics* (AIR-oh-die-NAM-iks).

First, an airplane must have a powerful engine. This *thrusts* it forward. Next, there must be enough force to push the plane up. Have you ever put your hand out the

Did You Know?
Some planes have more than one engine!

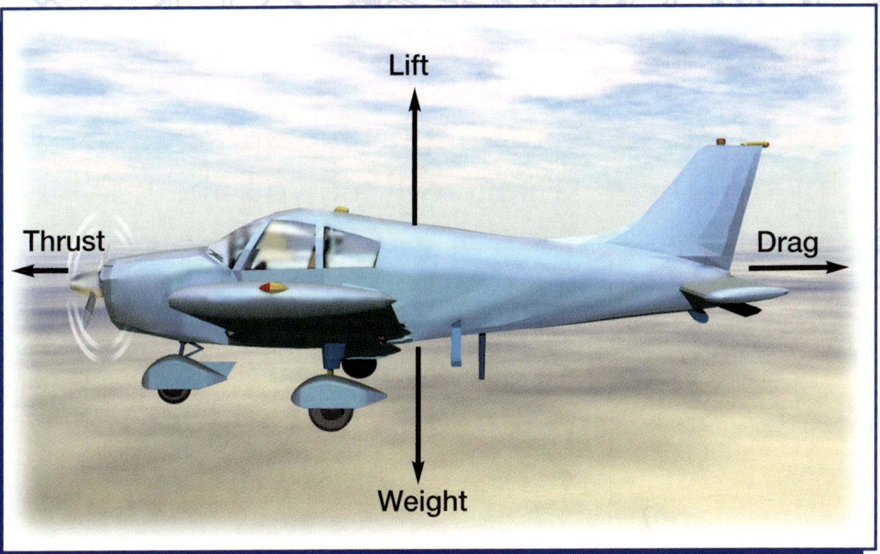

window of a moving car? Think about how the air pushed your hand upward. That is the force called *drag*. Finally, the wings change the drag into a force called *lift*. They do this by their shape and angle. This keeps the plane in the air.

Plane Diagram

Here are some important parts of a plane. The next page will tell you about them.

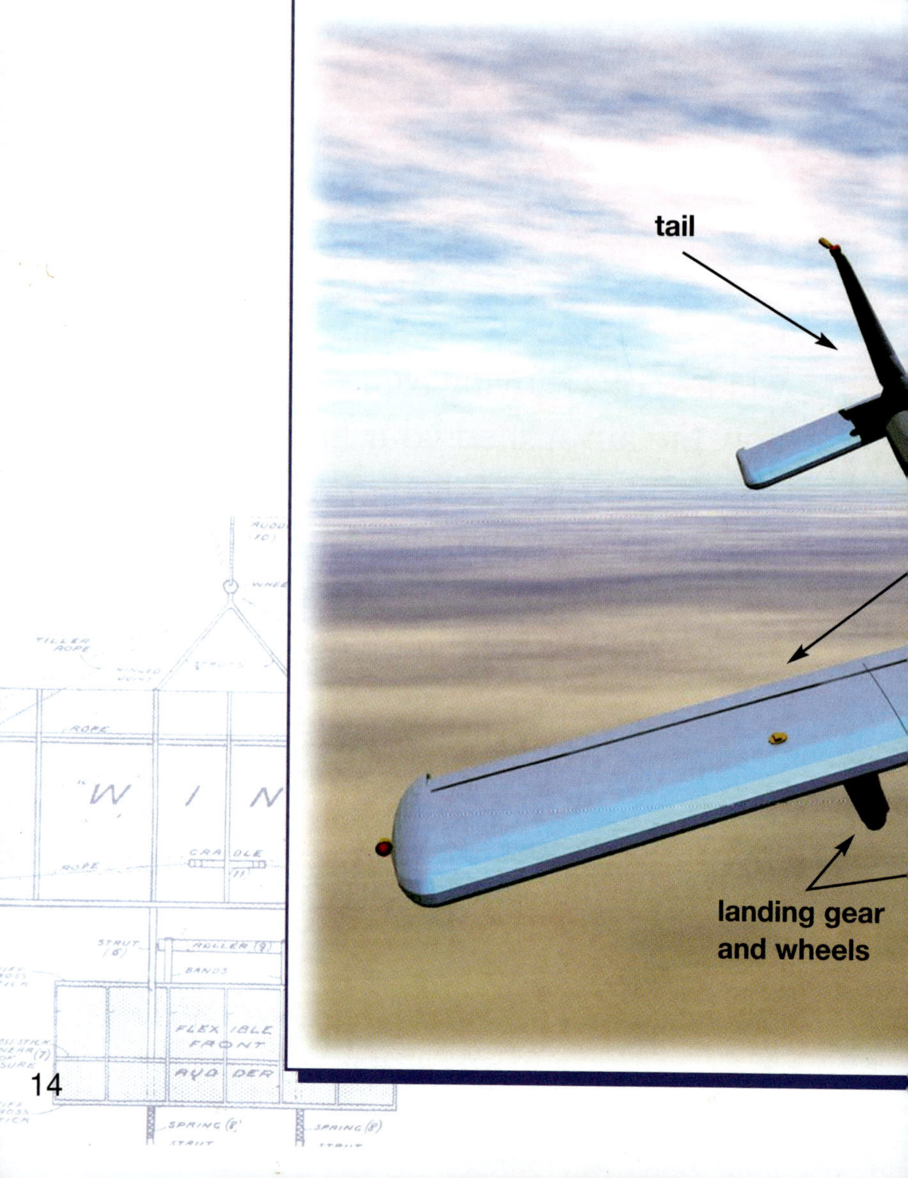

wings
fuselage

An airplane has many parts that help it fly. The body of the plane is called the *fuselage* (FYOO-suh-LAHZH). This is where the pilot and *passengers* sit. Parts of the *wings* are used to control the plane and keep it level. The wings lift the plane off the ground. Did you know that the *tail* of a

plane helps it fly? The tail makes the plane go up and down and helps it turn. *Landing gear* is under the body of the plane. When a plane lands, *wheels* drop down from the body. The wheels allow the plane to have a gentle landing.

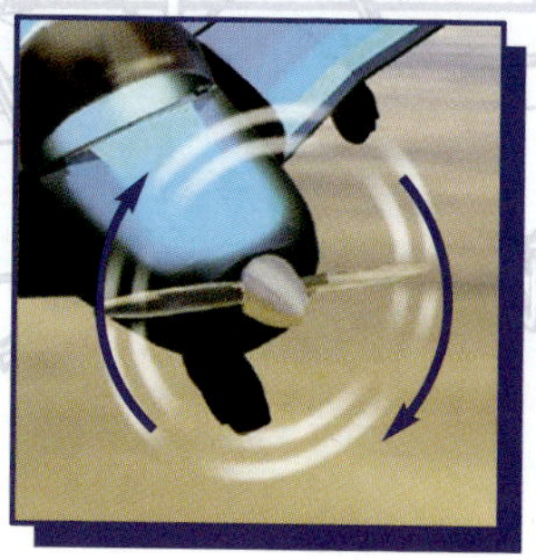

◀ Propeller planes

▼ Jet plane

Some airplanes use *propellers.* Propellers spin like fans. They are powered by the plane's engine.

Other planes use *jet engines.* The jet engine uses *fuel* and *air* to move the plane. This kind of engine is powerful. It makes the plane travel fast.

Over the years, plane designs have changed. The wings have been moved to different positions. Because of this, the airplane can take off on a shorter *runway.*

Pressurized Cabins

In earlier years, planes could not fly any higher than 10,000 feet. If planes went higher, people inside became dizzy and sometimes fainted. The higher a plane goes, the less air there is. Less air means less *oxygen*.

But pilots wanted to fly higher to avoid storms by climbing above them. Storms make flights very bumpy. This rough travel causes some passengers to get sick. So, planes were built to solve this problem.

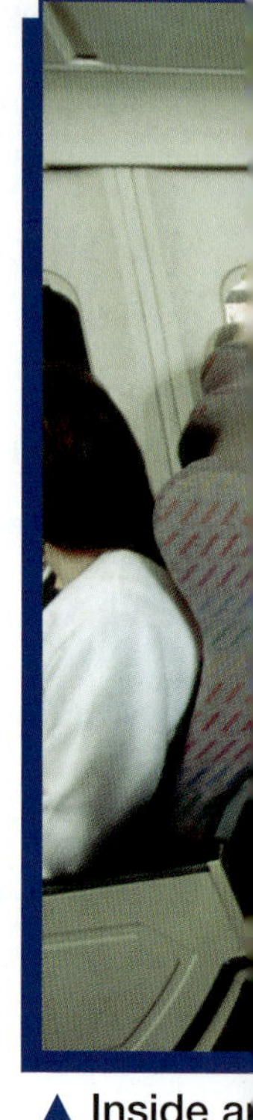

▲ Inside a airplane cabin ▼

Nowadays, the inside of a plane (the cabin) is *pressurized*. That means that air is pumped into the cabin. There is plenty of oxygen now. Airplanes can fly much higher, and passengers are much happier!

15,000
feet
3,000
feet
1,000
feet

Plane Transportation

Air travel has made life easier for most people. We can fly to faraway places in a short time. We take plane trips to visit family and friends and to go on vacations. Many people take planes regularly for business trips. Much mail travels by plane. Airplanes have become bigger, faster, and safer. They can travel day or night to almost anywhere in the world.

Glossary

aerodynamics　the study of the forces caused by objects moving through the air

cabin　the area inside an airplane where the passengers ride

commercial　used to make money; used to move goods

drag　the force created when an object pushes against air

fuel　something that is burned to make energy

fuselage　the body of an airplane

jet engine　powerful engine that releases gases under pressure from the rear vent of an object to move it

landing gear　the wheels and shock absorbing equipment below a plane

lift　the force, created by wings, that keep a plane in the air

military　the soldiers and protectors of a country

oxygen　a gas that has no color or taste, needed by people to breathe

passengers　people who travel in a plane or other type of transportation

pressurized　sealed so that normal air, including oxygen, can be pumped inside and not escape

propellers　blades, like a fan, used to provide thrust to move airplanes or boats

runway　a special road used by planes for taking off and landing

tail　back end of a plane that helps it to fly smoothly and keep steady in the air

thrust　the force causing forward movement

wing　part of a plane used to lift it off the ground and keep it level

Index

VERTICAL
RUDDER
(10)
WHEEL
TILLER
ROPE
TILLER
ROPE
HINGED
JOINT
STRUTS
HINGED
JOINT
WIRE
ROPE
MAIN FRAME
OF "WING"
PULLEY
"WING"
CRADLE
(11)
ROPE
ROPE
PULLEY
STRUT
(6)
ROLLER (9)
STRUT
(6)
BANDS
THIN
RIBS
FLEXIBLE

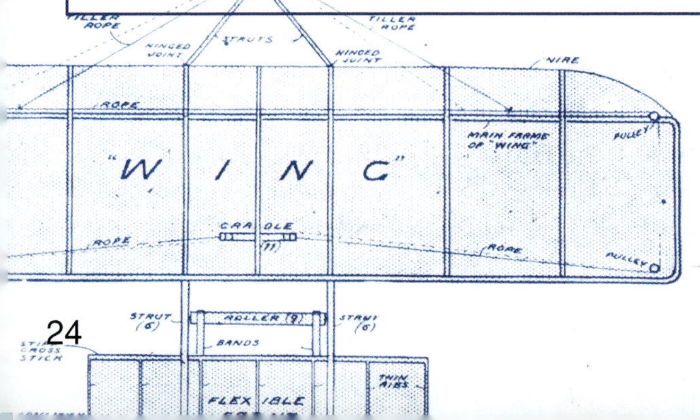